Our New Home
Immigrant Children Speak

OUr New HOMe
Immigrant Children Speak

edited by Emily Hearn and Marywinn Milne

Second Story Press

Library and Archives Canada Cataloguing in Publication

Our new home : immigrant children speak / edited by Emily Hearn
and Marywinn Milne.

ISBN 978-1-897187-32-6

1. Immigrant children—Canada—Biography—Juvenile literature.
2. Children of minorities—Canada—Biography—Juvenile literature.
3. Canada—Emigration and immigration—Psychological aspects—
Juvenile literature. I. Hearn, Emily, 1925- II. Milne, Marywinn, 1950-

FC104.O972 2007   j305.23086'9120971   C2007-905435-8

Cover and text design by Melissa Kaita
Front cover photo © Corbis
Map on page 2 by Phil Rutter

Printed and bound in Canada

*Second Story Press gratefully acknowledges the support of the Ontario Arts Council
and the Canada Council for the Arts for our publishing program. We acknowledge
the financial support of the Government of Canada through the
Book Publishing Industry Development Program.*

ONTARIO ARTS COUNCIL
CONSEIL DES ARTS DE L'ONTARIO

Canada Council   Conseil des Arts
for the Arts   du Canada

Published by
Second Story Press
20 Maud Street, Suite 401
Toronto, Ontario, Canada
M5V 2M5
www.secondstorypress.ca

CONTENTS

Many children participated in this project, not just the ones you see here. We would like to have all of them know how much we appreciate their honesty and depth of feeling in sharing their experiences with us. We dedicate this book to them.

INTroDUCTION

Have you and your family ever moved? Even if it was just to a new neighborhood in the same town or city, things probably felt pretty strange for a while, didn't they? The children whose letters you are about to read are telling you what happened to them when they left old friends and relatives behind in countries very far away from Canada. Not seeing them whenever they wanted to was hard. And it wasn't easy getting used to schools and customs that were so different from what they knew back home. Many had to learn English for the first time.

When we asked these children to help make this book they were eager to share their memories of earlier days and places by drawing pictures and writing about the things they felt when they were newcomers to Canada. You'll find that we have left their stories just the way they wrote them for you. We hope you enjoy meeting our new neighbors!

Emily Hearn
Marywinn Milne

1

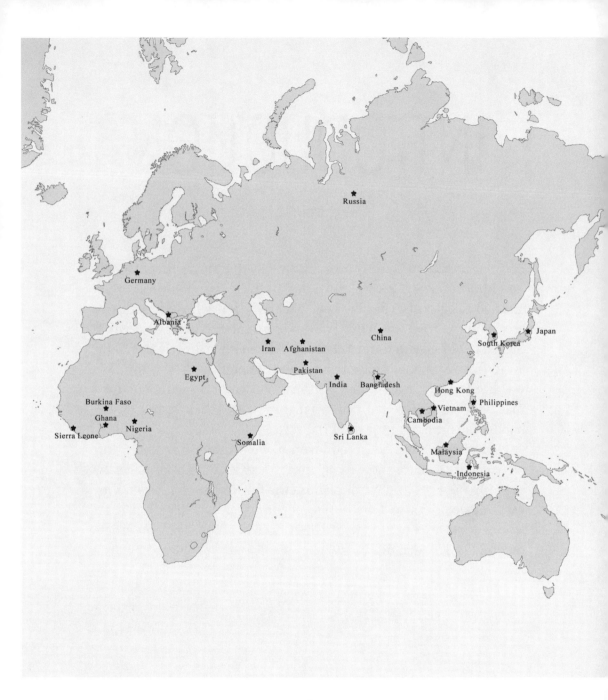

CANADA

★
United States

★
Mexico

★
Jamaica

★
Guyana

★
Argentina

WHere we came FROM

LEAVING

Imagine having your whole world change overnight — leaving everything and everybody familiar and landing somewhere completely new.

You'd feel like an alien from another planet. Children who have moved to Canada tell you about it.

Ikram Mohammed	**Somalia**
Abiram Surendra	**Sri Lanka**
Akshay Galia	**India**
Aneri Nanavaty	**India**
Asad Siddiqui	**Pakistan**
Ai Makino	**Japan**
Sidra Amjed	**Pakistan**
Celine Ooi	**Malaysia**
Eric Tran	**Cambodia**
John Thai	**Vietnam**
Justica Adjetey	**Ghana**
Dinesh	**Guyana**
Melodie Nguyen	**Vietnam**
Andrew Chung	**South Korea**
Paravinthan	**Sri Lanka**
Jathusa Kasinathar	**Sri Lanka/Germany**
Shirley Luong	**China**
Edward Chow	**Vietnam**

When I was born, Somalia was starting the Civil War. But it was as intense as now. The lake was still pure and people did not carry guns a lot. But two years later the bombs started firing and killed hundreds of people at a time. My mother fled to North America. A year later I was in an airplane heading away from Somalia. When I came to Canada it was mid January and the weather cold!! And I was in a short dress and sandals. My mom, she had to carry me from the airport. After a year in Canada I started to adjust and learn some English. But what I didn't know was that there wasn't any animals that I had in Somalia. I was very disappointed. But then I started to go to school and it was really fun. I forgot some of my language (Somalia) and started to learn more English.

Ikram
Somalia

Moving from Sri Lanka to Canada

I liked living in Sri Lanka because I had lots of friends and family members. My dad owned a shop in Sri Lanka so I get anything for free. My dad also owned chickens in Sri Lanka and I played with them. There was one chicken. When I put it in front of the radio it just listens to the radio. I also love Sri Lanka because it is fun playing cricket with my cousins. I did not want to leave Sri Lanka.

I don't like leaving Sri Lanka because I had lots of friends and family members. I didn't want to leave Sri Lanka because I didn't want to leave my family, friends and all the fun. I also left to Canada on my birthday. My dad did not want to go to Canada because he needs to handle the business.

I felt so scared when I am coming to Canada because I thought I couldn't hear when the plane took off. I was also happy because there was TV in the plane and I watched lots of movies. The scary thing is that when I went to the washroom I always thought that I will fall out of the plane's washroom. My favourite part was looking out of the window and watching the beautiful view from the plane.

Abiram
Sri Lanka

My family and I applied to go to Canada. After about one or two years we had all forgotten we even applied to go to Canada. Then, three years later, when I was eight, we got a letter that said you have been accepted to come to Canada. I was so happy for about two days, but then when it was actually time to go I felt so sad. My parents were really sad too. Then when I looked around I felt like crying because everyone was sad and really emotional. It was a time that I will never forget in my life.

Later that night, at about seven, they announced that the Air-India flight was about to leave. My whole family filled their eyes and hearts with tears, but my Dad told us to stay strong.

When the flight lifted off I was wondering where I was going to live, so I kept on asking my Mom, "Where are we going to stay?" "What are we going to do there?" (I am still wondering why we came here.) My Mom was still sad that we had to leave our motherland India, and her eyes still had tears.

Akshay
India

When I first found out we were immigrating, I was 5 years old and didn't know how to feel. I had heard stories of plane crashes so I was scared to even get on the plane. My dad told me, "Don't be afraid, just take God's name and everything will be just fine." And so it was.

Once we arrived in Toronto, Canada, my family and I met my aunt and uncle who had moved a year before us. Even though I had met them before in our hometown in India, I was shy. I soon got over it.

I had a dream that I was standing in the middle of the road and thinking, "What is to become of me? How will I survive? What lies upon me? What does the future have in store for me?"

My mom told me that I used to get disappointed when she went to job interviews and didn't get a job. I don't know how I could understand but somehow I did.

Aneri
India

When I Came to Canada

I am going to tell you about when I moved from Pakistan to Canada. When I was at Pakistan I was packing my clothes and my toys to Canada 2 days before moving. I got so many parties. I was talking on the computer to my cousins who were in India. I was getting ready what I am going to wear in whole travel from Pakistan to Canada. I stopped going to school because I was so busy. My mom was in a problem and she was saying, "How are the glass plates going in the suitcase?" and I said, "Cool down, Mom."

It was the last day in Pakistan. The suitcases were ready. The phone was so busy of my house. My cousins were saying goodbye to me and my family because they live far away from my house. My flight was 8:00 in the morning. I got to sleep at night and then I woke up at 4:00 at night and everyone was crying because we were going far away from them.

Asad
Pakistan

I am Ai and 7 years old. I was in the grade 1 of the elementary school in Japan. I arrived in Toronto, Canada on March 1st, 2005.

At the airport, I went to the washroom. The door of the washroom is short. So, I saw someone's legs. When I tried to look inside, my mother told me not to do it.

I had to go shopping everyday. I was told not to stay home alone in Canada when my mother goes out. Though I was very sleepy because of jet lag, my mother took me anywhere she went. It was very cold outside. Much colder than in Sendai (the name of the city where we live). But I saw some people sitting down on the street covered with snow. I asked my mother, "What are they doing?" Mother said, "They are the homeless, street people." "What are the homeless? What are street people?" I asked again. She explained, "They ask to give money." I had a little money, but this was given by my grandmother to get something for me in Canada. So, I could not give them my money.

My mother took me to a Korean Store. A clerk talked to me in Korean. I was surprised. "Do I look like a Korean?" I thought. But I can't tell Japanese from Korean in Toronto. And Chinese, too.

Ai
Japan

My family and I came from Pakistan. It's not clean there at all. Lots of people are poor and probably still are. You have to work very hard to get money but we were rich. So we didn't have to worry about that! My brothers and I were born in Pakistan.

My mom, brothers, some of my relatives and I lived in one big house in Pakistan while my dad was in Canada. He used to send us money so we can use it for our needs. My second oldest brother and I used to have disputes. It was so much fun living with my whole family.

When I moved to Canada almost everything was better than in Pakistan like the roads, places and lots more. The only problem was the people in school! They weren't very nice and I thought they could have been nicer! They called me names and made fun of me. I missed my old friends back in Pakistan who were nice and kind to me. I cried and cried but didn't lose hope for friends. I moved to Canada for education.

Sidra
Pakistan

13

When I was in Malaysia, I didn't feel safe. Malaysia had lots of bad people and lots of burglars. My parents did not allow me and my brothers to play outside alone because it is not safe.

Malaysia has lots of beaches and beautiful fishes. There is a beach named Pulau Redang. It is my favourite beach. The sea is clean and the air is fresh. There are so many birds flying around. It was a wonderful place. I saw lots of colourful fishes and big corals. I also fed small fishes plain bread. The fishes were all surrounding me. They were tickling my feet. I was having so much fun but it was time to go. It was the last time I went to this great place because I was going to Canada soon. I wish someday I could still come to this beach.

After two years in Canada I felt great! Canada is a wonderful country. I like Canada more than Malaysia because I don't have to worry about robbers and scary things. But I still like Malaysia because it's my home country. I am learning lots of new things in Canada. It's great to be in a new country and learn new things.

Celine
Malaysia

I am 11 years old and my parents are from Cambodia. My parents came here because of peace and in Cambodia they had lots of war and taking over everybody's house shelter. My dad had to run all the way from Cambodia to Thailand. My mom ran all the way to Vietnam and after my dad ran there. My mom and her family was poor before my mom's cousins were already at Canada and gave the money to my mom and her family to go on the plane. After they came my mom and her family got clothes and lots of money. Then that's when my mom and dad met together.

Eric
Cambodia

My name is John and I come from Vietnam. My parents came to Canada becuase there was a war. South Vietnam and North Vietnam had a war. Americans has help Vietnam to have victory in wars. Then we had a war with French people. Then after a few years I have been born. Then we had more wars coming that was when we had an idea. People that was scared goes on the boat to Canada and the US. Then the people who wants to be in the war stays.

John
Vietnam

My Journey to Canada

My mother and I came to Canada because my father was here. My father wanted my mother to come here because he was here. My mother couldn't get a good job in Ghana. In my country there are no jobs so my father came back to Ghana to marry my mother. After they got married months later they both came to Canada. They came here in 2003. When they left my older sister was taken care of me because she was not going to school. When my mother got a job she wanted me to come here so that I can go to school. In my country you go to school only if your family has money. If your family does not have money to pay for school you can't go to school. My mother said if she gets a good job she will go to my country Ghana for a visit and come back.

Justica
Ghana

Dark Home

I am 11 years old. My family and I came to Canada in 2001. I will tell you about my family's past life. We were rich in Guyana but we had a very dangerous life.

Almost ever night thieves and bandits would sneak pass our securities and threaten my parents. They would demand our money and gold. My dad was a goldsmith and my mom was a teacher. I will tell you about one of the worst attacks we had. It was a very dark night.

My dad was in his workshop, when all of a sudden someone with a mask points a gun at him and said, "Open the door, otherwise I will shoot." My dad was very frightened so he had no choice but to open the door. At this time, I was about 3-4 years old so my mom hid me and my brother while she quietly called the cops. By the time the thieves open the door, they were surround by the police.

The cops arrested all four of them and gave them 11 years in prison. So by now you probably know why I came to Canada, for protection and safety.

Dinesh
Guyana

Vietnamese Immigrants

My parents and sister have been through a lot years ago. 23 years ago before my sister was born, my parents tried to escape from Vietnam and got caught by the Vietnamese police. They were thrown in jail and spent a few years in there. That was over two decades ago. That's when my sister Anh was born and turned 2, my parents tried again. This time, they managed to get on a small boat. There were a lot of people on that small boat, about over 30 excluding kids. They had to survive 3 days (I think) without food and water. And the boat was crowded. Then they landed in Philippines and lived there for 2 years. Then they moved to Canada and lived here, but moved a couple of times. Then they had me and 3 years later, my brother. Then we had to move because the apartment was too small. And we moved here and we lived here ever since.

Melodie
Vietnam

My Parents' Hard Life

This is about my parents who had a hard life in Canada. So my mom and dad had come to Canada with my mother's mom and my father came alone with his wife, which is my mom. My mom came with her mother, 3 sisters, and 1 brother. When my mom came everyone in the family went to go buy a house or a condo in an apartment. My parents had enough money to buy a condo in an apartment. So they lived there. They bought all the supplies they needed and they lived for a good while. When my mom got pregnant and had a baby it was a boy. I was so cute. My parents bought me a lot of stuff and I have most of the stuff in my house right now. My parents left South Korea because they were afraid of wars or fights against North Korea. So my parents had a hard life because they did not know that English would be so hard. They had difficult times when they had to speak English. They knew some English but not a lot. So when I wanted McDonald's they barely knew how to order.

So they had to try reading it or pointing to it. Then they would have to pay. My dad had a hard time finding a job too. But he finally found one as a tour guide and now he is a manager of the Toronto branch of Skyline Tours. The main branch is in Vancouver. So my dad had a job and he always went somewhere so he was almost gone from the house. I had no time with him a lot. It was hard because he needed money to support us but he was paid little bit around $100 a month. Then he got a better job offer with Korean people who would be able to help him in English because they have been living here for around 15 years. So after that it became a lot easier for us and that was the end of the problems.

Andrew
South Korea

The Escape

My uncle used to live in Sri Lanka. As you know the civil war was going on. All boys 12 and older would be taken to fight. Lots of people didn't want to go but they had no choice.

To escape, my uncle used a false passport which cost $10,000 to go to Africa. There he stayed for four weeks. Then he went to Belgium but got caught there and was sent to jail.

He had to pay another $10,000 to get out. After that he took a trailer to England, got caught and was sent to jail for two weeks. He paid $10,000 and got out but to go to England he paid another $10,000.

As you know Canada and England are non-violent countries and so they don't put you in jail so he paid his last $10,000, came to Canada and claimed refugee status. So that's the story of the escape!

Paravinthan
Sri Lanka

My name is Jathusa. I am in Grade 4 and will be 10 years old in June. I came to Canada with my brother and my mom 18 months ago. My mom and dad were born in Sri Lanka. It's very hot there. I have never been there. My Mom and dad left because fighting was going on.

My little brother and I were born in Germany. In Germany the kids at school all made fun of me. They talked about me worse than bullying. They made me cry alot. They called me chocolate and asked me how come I was brown. I also wore glasses so they called me a word that sounded like glasses but meant cobra snake in German. They said the cobra's big hood looked like my glasses.

I was sad my Dad had to go back to Sri Lanka and get better papers but I was glad to leave Germany. In my school here there are nice people. My friends are from different countries like Sri Lanka, India, Africa and Canada. We are still waiting for my Dad to come. We miss him alot.

Jathusa
Sri Lanka/Germany

Shirley
China

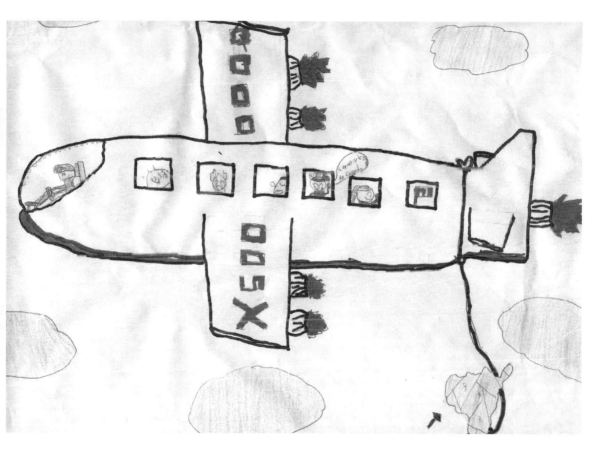

Edward
Vietnam

DIFFerences

Children from such countries as Afghanistan, India, Nigeria, and China describe where they used to live and remember what they were taught and how they played. How different it all was then and how different it is now, especially if they weren't used to the shivery winter temperatures.

Fereshta Karimi	**Afghanistan**
Sawayz Sayed	**Afghanistan**
Hamza Quershi	**Pakistan**
Axel Smith	**Argentina**
Edison Tang	**Hong Kong**
Maureen Doherty	**Sierra Leone/Burkina Faso**
Christina Lapytskaia	**Russia**
Chris Zhu	**China**
Yao Da	**China**
Bo Chen Han	**China**
Brian Wu	**China**
Kimberly Cross	**Jamaica**
Jesutoyitan Adeyemo	**Nigeria**
Vivek Chachcha	**India**
Dipan	**India**
Bhim Pandya	**India**
David Kwak	**South Korea**
JiHoon Kang	**South Korea**
John Yoo	**South Korea**
Ryan Huh	**South Korea**
Jeff Jun	**South Korea**
Samuel	**Indonesia**
Stephy Huang	**China**
Michelle Li	**China**
Vidhi Patel	**India**
Diana Lewars	**Jamaica**
Vaishnavi Patel	**India**

When I was in Afghanistan lots of bad things had happened to my family and my cousins. There was these people coming. They were all bad people. They thought that they were the boss of Afghanistan. When they had came they didn't let people show their faces. They had to cover it, even me. When I was so small they were being rude to everyone. The bad people had to make them eat only a little bit of food. They had to eat bread with water. They did have food to eat but the others didn't let them to eat the food that they had with them. They were making fun of the people of how they had to eat their food. I felt sorry for myself and my family, also cousins. We all felt so scared. We didn't know what to do. We all tried to escape but we didn't. They were all everywhere. They had their guns in their hands and they actually were trying to shoot us but we didn't let them we were all hiding in our houses. Our houses were so poor. It wasn't made properly. They couldn't afford any other houses that were all properly made. We all felt sorry for ourselves and other people that were there with my family.

Fereshta
Afghanistan

29

Back home in Afghanistan people worked hard for money. 10 year old children had to work and little kids had to be in the army. Most of the children had to be a worker and had to work hard. Most of our houses were handmade and built by hard clay. There were alot of Afghan dogs and they are the world's most strongest dogs in the world and they attack by their chest and one swipe of their powerful claws you are dead. There was alot of war and there still is. When the war came, about one hundred people died when the other country attacked. There was alot of tanks and army stuff. When I first came to Canada, I was scared because I didn't have any friends to play with. I also didn't speak English. Now I have friends to play with and I can speak English really well.

Sawayz
Afghanistan

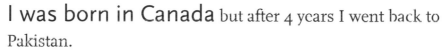

I was born in Canada but after 4 years I went back to Pakistan.

First of all I will talk about how my life was when I was in Pakistan and how my school was there. My life in Pakistan was really good. I was really happy. Over there the main sport that everyone including me was cricket even though ground hockey was and is the national game of Pakistan. Now I will tell you about how my school was there. My school was really good. In Pakistan in the schools the studies were really hard for example some of the things I'm learning in Grade 7 in Canada I learned it in grade 2 in Pakistan. In Pakistan in the schools the teachers were allowed to hit us but I think it was a good thing because if you got hit once trust me you'd never do it again.

Now I will talk about when I found out that I was going back to Canada and how I felt in school and how it was and

I'll also tell you about how I felt after a little while in Canada. When I came to school I had no friends and I didn't know much English but in some days I made a very nice friend named Miraj who was new in Canada and he was from India. My school was really good but the studies were pretty easy comparing to Pakistan. The teachers were really good and they didn't hit here. After a little life in Canada everything was good but I would still like to visit Pakistan.

Hamza
Pakistan

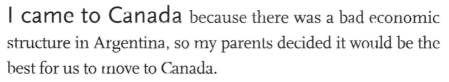

I came to Canada because there was a bad economic structure in Argentina, so my parents decided it would be the best for us to move to Canada.

If I ever wanted to go outside from my house in Argentina I always had to be watched by either my mom or my dad. I always felt like a prisoner in my front yard behind a big iron fence.

Now living in Canada, I can go outside; I can ride my bike and I do not have to be watched by my parents.

Before I came to Canada I had never seen these white powdery cold stuff which were so called snow.

If I was ever going back to Argentina I would like to visit my grandparents' home in a little town outside of Buenos Aires called Lincoln.

Axel
Argentina

In the leisure time I usually played soccer with my uncle and brother. But I didn't know why I played this game worse than them. Sometimes we rode a bicycle together so my uncle usually bought some drinks for us. Though we only had three people but we could play very happy.

Every night I always talked with my mother before sleeping. We talked about that day all the things that happened. Though we had different things happen in everyday, but I can talk one thing with you. "Today is holiday so in the morning I go to the club with my brother and classmates to play many things such as basketball, tennis and bowling. But while I was playing basketball, my leg was wounded so I just sat on the chair, looked at they played, then we went back home." I hope to talk to my mother everyday but I am living in Canada now.

In the airport my mother unceasingly cried, all my relatives very grieve. Then I went away. Though my father went with me but I as before very grieve.

Edison
Hong Kong

The country I came from is called Burkina Faso. It is very hot there and it doesn't snow there. That's because it is very, very close to the equator. The kind of clothing my family wore there was we wore African clothing, skirts, jeans, shorts, tops, and other things that you would were in the Summer.

There are only 2 seasons in Burkina Faso. Those seasons are the dry season and the wet season. This country is in West Africa. Usually, it's very hot there, but the only time it is cold there is when it's raining. We only stayed there for 4 years. When I came to Canada, I was 7 years old. I've only been in Canada for 2 and a half years.

When I first came to Canada, I was very curious. It was so big! I tasted so many different foods and saw so many different people. I also wore different clothing. I was amazed by all the languages I heard! I was also amazed by all the different cultures.

When I saw the buildings, I couldn't believe my eyes! When I heard about all the different celebrations, I was so exited! The music I heard was very sensational. I felt like I would live happily, and I still do. I was very proud of my family. I was very interested in how the schools were going on.

As soon as I found out about libraries, I begged my parents to take me to a public library, to get my library card. When I went to my first barbecue, I was extremely excited. But after I heard about seasons I prepared myself. Then, I started making friends with different kinds of people.

The day I first saw snow, I was amazed by its crystal-colour beauty. I had good friends and neighbours. There were so many TV channels, that I didn't want to stop watching TV. When I found out that English is the main language, I was very happy. I loved the things that I had and found out about.

Maureen
Sierra Leone/Burkina Faso

(Maureen grew up in Sierra Leone, then spent four years in Burkina Faso (in Africa) and then came to Canada.)

July 1, 1993. Christina's born. Not crying, not sleeping, just lying down and examining the place. I was born in St. Petersburg, Russia. I grew up there. It was always fun going to figure skating lessons. Everytime I saw a streetcar I would complain to my mom and ask her if we could go on it. I was very excited when I finally did, since I always rode in the car. I had a dog but he died because he ate some glass or dirt. He used to give me piggyback rides. I also had a cat but we gave her to a friend when we moved to Canada.

I was six when we moved. When we came here we stayed in a hotel by the airport. Everytime a plane would come an alarm went off. I could hardly sleep. Then we went to stay by Spadina. My brother and I took Tae Kwon Do. Roma already took it in Russia but I was just starting. It was alot of fun, and I had alot of friends there. In a couple of years I went to a tournament where I fought all boys. It wasn't fair since he hit my arm when I blocked his kick and they counted that as a point. Because of that I got second place.

Christina
Russia

On the first day in Canada I felt it hard to get comfortable with the area because everything is so different. The space in Canada is much larger than the ones in Shan Dong. There are only a limited amount of farmland in Shan Dong but there are more farmland and larger ones in Canada. One of the reasons why I like Canada is because it is very clean. Also there are more people and more friends to make.

In my opinion the education in Canada is a lot better than the one in Shan Dong. Furthermore there are only apartments in Shan Dong.

As much as the differences between Shan Dong and Canada there are many similarities too. One of the similarities is the pollution in the two places. There are also cars in Shan Dong. The transportation in the two places are very familiar. They are familiar because they both have trains, cars and buses.

On the first day of school I thought it was hard to make friends and understand the teacher. However when I learned about the education system in Canada it is actually easier than I thought it would've been. After the first recess of the day I was introduced to many other students and I ended up making friends with most of them. These are my feelings to the first few weeks of Canada.

Chris
China

I came from China at 2005 the 21 of November. I miss my home. In China there is no snow and in Canada there is. School here don't need money and in China they do. If the teacher said something some I understand some I don't. Here I never seen fighting but in China there always is. I made some friends — Jiang Jiang, Wenbin, Wenfeng. In Canada we have a lot of subjects and in China we have a few. In China class we don't have computers and in Canada they do. This place is a good place to live. In Art here we can do stuff like craft but in China they didn't. In China we play soccer.

Yao
China

My First Experiences to Canada

I came to Canada on September 29th, 2002 from China. I was only six. I was really excited to go a new country. I lived in an island called Hainan. People speak two languages there: Mandarin and Hainanese. Canada was totally different than China. Canada is mostly cold and snowy, but from the part of China that I came from, it was always hot. So it was my first time seeing snow. Snow was very new to me but after awhile I learned to make snow angels, snowmen and throw snowballs. One thing I hate about snow is that it's very cold and we have to dress warmly meaning wearing a lot of clothes. In China all we have to wear are t-shirts and pants. When it's cool we only have to wear a sweater and pants; we never had to wear big jackets, boots, snow pants or even mittens! This was very new but I like snow!

Celebrations and holidays in Canada are different than celebrations and holidays in China. No one celebration or holiday is the same, except for the New Year. I think that's because of all the different religions. Christmas is because of Christianity, Remembrance Day is because to remember the Canadian Soldiers. Canada's summer breaks and winter breaks are longer than China's too. Chinese students and workers sometimes have make-up days like going to school on Saturdays and Sundays, and then have the holiday. Even traffic rules are different; in most parts of China people just cross the road whenever they want. Canada is a bit organized. Canadian money is also is also different; not only the style and pictures, the worth of it is also different. One dollar of Canadian money is equalled to 6.80 dollar of Chinese money. Canada is totally different than China. I really like Canada, but I like China too. Now that I know how to speak English, I'm trying to enjoy Canada even more. I had very good experiences first coming to Canada!

Bo Chen
China

When I was in China whenever it's a holiday a lot of friends called me out to play or some relatives invited me to go shopping and eat food. Lunar New Year was even happier. We finished our meal in the morning and went to our relatives and friends for blessings! We got red pocket money during the blessings. After blessings I was invited to go out to play. At night, my whole family must go back to home town for dinner. After the dinner we played mahjong, chess and started fireworks. We were all very happy. Apart from Lunar New Year it was also very happy for me to play with my school mates.

Brian
China

I relocated from Jamaica about 4 months ago. It was very hard leaving my friends behind. However, it was very exciting moving to a new country with my family, after all, it's one of the world's largest continents.

I have grown to like the Canadian school system although it is different from Jamaica's. I really like my teacher Mrs. Koivuranta. She is very creative. I was amazed while getting to know Canada how some of their celebrations are also celebrated in Jamaica, such as: Teachers' Day, Children's Day and Parents' Day. On Teachers' Day in Jamaica, we usually give our teachers mugs, flowers and cake. I have just started to learn French but I am pretty good at it, I just need to improve on some skills and vocabulary.

In Jamaica, our national dish is ackee and saltfish, and the saltfish is actually imported from Canada. The colours of our flag are yellow, green and black which mean, "The sun shineth; the land is green and the people are strong and creative."

My favourite Jamaican fruits are ripe bananas, oranges and starapples. Two of the main resources of our island that catch the eyes of our many tourists are our white, sandy beaches and our warm, tropical climate.

Kimberly
Jamaica

Coming to Canada!!!

I landed in Canada on the afternoon of August 8th 2002. I came from a country called Nigeria which is located in the west side of Africa. I came to Canada with my family of five, because my dad said it was an opportunity for me and my siblings to become successful people in life.

There are few differences between Canada and Nigeria. The school systems are different. The school system in Nigeria allows the student to be caned if the student misbehaves or if the student does something wrong. In Canada such things are not allowed. If the student misbehaves the student could get a detention, get suspended or get expelled depending on what he or she did. The Nigerian School system puts students in classes according to what their report cards say, in other words, their performances. For example, if they were in grade eight and were very smart, they would be put in 8A and if they weren't smart at all they were put in 8Z. In Canada students are randomly put in classes and according to their age.

Another difference between Canada and Nigeria are the houses. The houses in Nigeria are very easy to own. The owner buys the land, then the hired contractors build the houses. They could also just buy the houses from someone else. In Canada, people who want to own houses have to pay mortgages for a long period of time before they own a house. This doesn't occur in Nigeria.

Coming to Canada was a very fun and exciting change for me. Although I miss Nigeria, I have learnt to adjust and have come to feel that Canada is just home for me.

Jesutoyitan
Nigeria

When I had arrived in Canada I was sure I could have fainted. In my country there is a population of millions and millions and in Canada wherever I go I see less people. I feel the same way about pollution. In India the pollution is about a hundred times worse than here!

The first school I went to was a "creative" school meaning it had different ways of making one learn something. The current school I am going to a school with "excitement" where I learn different and fun activities. In both of my schools and outdoor life, my skills have helped me so I can be considered to be a "dude." What I mean is, being a kid who can hang out with anyone I want, like a guy who can be considered a "cool" friend.

Less pollution, less population, friends with good habits, school with more extracurricular activities and places with more security are some of the ways that my life has changed for the better. But some things like my family and my culture stayed the same and will never change.

Vivek
India

When I was 6 years old I moved to Canada. I only spoke Hindi. I was coming to Canada. I felt excited. On my first day of school I felt sad. On the second day of my school I was happy. Then I had lots of friends and I was happy. Everyday I had lots of fun with my friends. In Canada's winter it was too cold. In India it was hot. If I go back to India I will not feel like coming back to Canada because there is so much hot and I like sunny days.

Dipan
India

My name is Bhim and I'm in Grade 4. I was born in India in 1995. My family came to Canada so my sister and I could learn English. My country has lots of people. It is so hot with lots of rainfall. In India there are no supermarkets like Food Basics or No Frills. They are all outdoors. When it rains they cover everything with a big tent. My classroom had 53 children and if you are not concentrating the teachers throw a duster at you. I like my school here and in India. My favourite Indian meal is Parata Masala. Here I like deep dish burritos from Taco Bell and New York Fries.

In Canada on the first day of school I went home for lunch and I didn't know what door to go back in. It was very scary. That day I didn't want to come to school because I didn't know how to speak English.

Soon I got two friends called Jainil and Deep. I would like to visit India after some years. In India I had a really big house where I lived with my grandma, my grandpa, my mom, my dad, my aunt, my sister and me. It was more fun in India. In Canada I live on the 7th floor in an apartment building.

Bhim
India

I like Canadian schools. In Korea there are 40-50 people in one class and when I see the desks there are many knife carvings on the desks. So when I write some words on paper, the words writing is strange, because of the knife carvings. But in Canada, the school desks are clean. P.S there are no knife carvings. In Canada my favourite thing is the trees, because in Korea there are no more trees. But in Canada there are many trees. Some times I miss my family and my friends. Especially I miss my dog. His name is Gi - Goo.

David
South Korea

I think Canada has good air and I like good air. I like the people because some people are so kind. I like this school, but I miss my house. I miss my school and I miss my friends (my pets too.) Korea has bad air, and schools are small, and inside it is dirty. But everything is ok. My house in Korea was an apartment. My house was on the 17th floor. In Canada, I live in a house with my father, my mother and my brother. In Korea, my family are 7.

JiHoon
South Korea

I like it here in Canada, because I can learn English. It is different in Canadian schools at recess time, because we can go out and play but in Korean schools at recess time we can't go out and play.

John
South Korea

For me, Canada is very big and calm. What I like about Canada is that in the school teachers give me the notebooks for free. Also, what I like about Canada is that in the school teachers don't hit students. A different thing about Canada and Korea, which is the land I was from, is that Canada has more houses than apartments. But Korea has more apartments than houses.

Ryan
South Korea

I think Korea and Canada are the same because people are live in big cities. I think Canada and Korea are different because Canada has balcony at apartments and Korean apartments don't usually have balconies. In Korea I had lots of classes at school, more than here. I don't like it here because here it is too cold. But I want to live here because still I want to learn English.

Jeff
South Korea

What I miss in Indonesia

I lived in Indonesia and I miss my apartment building, my toys, TV shows, my cousins, my friends, the foods in Indonesia and the other stuff. But my dad goes to Indonesia to do his work in Indonesia but my mom, sisters and I call my dad to Indonesia and my dad said, "Do you want me to buy you anything in Indonesia?" and we sometimes say, "No" or "Yes, I want something in Indonesia. I want…" and my dad always comes back to Canada again to meet us.

Samuel
Indonesia

On the first day that I came to Canada my family and I were very confused but luckily we received help by our uncle. Our uncle came and picked us up from the airport. Afterwards he drove us to his house to stay for a while. The roads in Canada are very different from the roads in Guang Zhou. The houses and apartments didn't look like the ones in Guang Zhou. There are more open spaces in Canada than at Guang Zhou. In my opinion the drivers in Canada drive a lot faster than the ones in Guang Zhou. The transportation part is very difficult because you have to drive everywhere. This is how I thought about Canada on the first day here.

Stephy
China

My name is Michelle. My Chinese name is Wan Ying
Li. I am 10 years old in grade 4. I lived in China for 8 1/2 years.
I came to Canada on June 15th, 2003 with my mom and dad.
I don't know why I had to come to Canada but my mom told
me that Canada is much better than China. Also my mom
had reminded me that I'm going to have a much better life in
Canada. At that time I was not so sure that I was really going
to have a better life in Canada.

When my family and I reached Canada I was really really
nervous because I didn't know anybody or any English at all.
After a few months it was time to go to my first school in
Canada. Before that time I had learned some English and I
was proud of myself. My first school was Agincourt Jr. P.S.
It is smaller than the school I have now which is Woburn
Jr. P. S. I still like it! At Agincourt school all the teachers are
very kind. They made me feel better if I was so nervous about
something. I learned so many things in that school and I had
promised myself that I would never forget all I had learned
and especially the wonderful school I have been to. Well, my
Chinese school is so different than my Agincourt school.
When you are nervous about something, the teachers in my

Chinese school make you feel much worse and if you don't know something or you did something wrong, they used a big fat stick to hit you in the hand or your head! Once my teacher hit my friend so badly that my friend's head even had blood. My Chinese teacher never ever said, "sorry" to her and never told her parents! You have to wake up at 6:00 o'clock in the morning to get ready for school because school is starting at 6:30 a.m. When it is recess time, we could only stay in one spot and skip rope or stand there watching people skip rope. The worst part is that you can't even talk with your friends! The teachers give you so much homework that you don't even have time to play after school and when the teachers get mad at you, they could yell at you and even say bad words to you! Sometimes other students had made their own teacher a gift. The teacher would say they didn't want it or they just throw it in the garbage or gave it to somebody else! The whole school would only have 3 or 4 gym classes or art classes in a month.

Michelle
China

Vidhi
India

Diana
Jamaica

Vaishnavi
India

adJUSTING

Bundling up in snowsuits and playing winter sports in their new home warmed up children on snowy days. Meeting new friends at school who could speak their language made a big difference for children facing big changes. But learning to speak English was hard!

Maira Hannan	**Pakistan**
Siddarth Patel	**India**
Wenbin Jiang	**China**
Padina Abmadieh-Bondar	**Iran**
Bo Chen Han	**China**
Rachael Jung	**South Korea**
Ai Makino	**Japan**
Sara Jang	**South Korea**
Neda Mortaji	**Iran**
Arash Barati	**Iran**
Ina Kasmollari	**Albania**
Martha Acosta Bernal	**Mexico**
Abiram Surendra	**Sri Lanka**
Yuki Makino	**Japan**
Rachael Jung	**South Korea**
Hinako Hosoya	**Japan**

Hi. My name is Maira and I love to write stories. I even like to talk about myself and my past.

When people listen to my past they laugh and they want me to tell them again. Well, when I first came to Canada it was snowing and I had never seen snow before so I didn't know what it was. Anyway I am from Pakistan. Pakistan is a very warm country so I thought snow was too cold. First I thought snow was soap because I was seven years old.

People right now think I am 10 but I am really 11. The first day I went to school I was suppose to be in grade two. But since I did not know any english they put me in grade one. When they showed me to my class I did not want to go in, so the teacher called the principal. The principal was so fat and her voice was so deep. She said hello in a nice voice but I heard her say it like this "haaaalllllooooooo!" I was really scared so I ran to my dad. Then he had to stay with me for the whole day. And that's the story of me.

Maira
Pakistan

Hi. My name is Siddarth.

I am 10 years old and in Grade 4. I came to Canada on March 15, 2001. I was born in India and I lived in a house in Baroda. It is very hot and there are many earthquakes in India. In my school our teacher was mean and if you didn't do the homework the teacher would hit us with a ruler. My favourite Indian food is palak panir.

It is hard to settle in Canada because of the seasons. The first days of school were hard because it was hard for me to speak English. After one month I started to make new friends. One friend is Siddarth K. He and I both like cricket. At first I didn't like Canada because it was so cold in winter. Since then I have learned winter can be fun. Now I like to go sleigh riding and build snow forts and snowmen and I might learn to skate.

Siddarth
India

I came from China two years and two months ago. When I first came to here I feel cold. In the night I can't sleep because the time between Canada and China is different. Sometimes I cry because I don't have any friends and I miss my grandma and grandpa.

I am better after I go to school because I meet my first friend in Canada. His name was Benoit Chow and I meet one friend. He was my neighbourhood in China because I don't know English at all so I don't really like to talk to other students. Sometimes some students will make fun of me because I don't know English but I don't know English so I don't understand what they are saying so I don't care at all. In class I don't understand what our teacher is talking about so I don't have to do the homework excerpt for my ESL homework. ESL homework is easy to do so after all I don't have to do much work. That was one good thing if you don't know English.

After school usually I finish my homework first, then watch TV and play computer. Sometimes I will go to the park.

Wenbin
China

I walked in the classroom completely green of what was going to happen. A lady approached me with a smile and said to me kindly, "What is your name?" No reply. All I remember was quivering as a tear slowly swayed down my cheek. A little girl came to me and said (in Farsi), "Hi, my name is Miriam. What is your name?" That moment I felt so calm I thought to see someone who will help me pull through, a friend. Of course I was wrong. Sometimes kids can be very cruel. For the first week everyone was around me trying to make friends but after that I was sitting alone in a corner. After that kids started to come around but just to make fun of me. It seemed that I didn't understand what they were saying but I understood every word. I use to wish everyday.

In Grade 5, I moved to a new house so I changed my school. The kids at this school were a lot better and I understood a bit of English so it was easier to make friends. I was soon in a group of friends with 4 other girls. Things were better but still being the new kid at a new school people felt the right to pick on me. It wasn't until grade 7 where I started to like things and be glad to live in Canada. Now I have 4 major best friends and am good friends with almost everyone in grade 8. I have visited Iran every summer since I've been here but I still feel really sad thinking of all the things I missed with my cousins.

Padina
Iran

The first day of school was very scary. I didn't know anyone and nobody knew me. I was in second grade. My school was called Rose Ave. When we came in the classroom my mom and dad talked to the teacher while I sat on the carpet. Every pair of eyes were staring at me. I had butterflies in my stomach. My teacher's name was Mrs. Soares. She was very nice. She introduced me to another Chinese girl, but the girl did not speak Mandarin like me. She spoke Cantonese. Her name was Vivian. She became my first best friend. Mrs. Soares had to get a translator every time I didn't understand something. I was very embarrassed. I learned English very quickly. Within a month I was good at speaking English. I even tried to read books. My favourites that time were picture books, like Clifford. That's how my love of reading started. Now I like to read more complicated books like the series of

"Harry Potter." I also learned there were lots of different kinds of people in the world like Chinese, Japanese, Vietnamese, Indian, British and many others. In China it was mostly Chinese people and very few people from other countries. I realized Canadian's elementary education is a lot easier than Chinese elementary education in different ways.

Bo Chen
China

On April 1, 2005 a beautiful young girl named Rachael arrived in Vancouver, Canada for the first time. She couldn't speak English except for 'Hi.' Because of this she felt very alone. She felt that everyone else was a genius because they could speak English. She was a very shy girl so she didn't want to go to school but her mother yelled at her for 3 hours. So the next day she had to go to school.

The first day is hard for everyone but for Rachael it was a nightmare. Everyone was walking up to her to meet the new student. Everyone was asking her different questions but all she could say was 'hi.' They all laughed at her and she didn't know what else to do so she started laughing too. The first bell rang and everyone went to their class but Rachael couldn't go anywhere because she didn't know where to go. Finally a teacher found her and took her to the office. Eventually she went to her art class. Art class seemed pretty easy to her because all she had to do was draw. Sometimes she looked beside her at her classmate's picture because she couldn't understand what the teacher was saying. But the next class which was science she got a headache because she was so lost. She thought it's OK because she saw the students saying 'hi' to the teacher so she said 'hi' too but the teacher asked her, "Are you a new student?" and she said, "Hi." The teacher said, "What's your name?" and again she said, "Hi." For the whole class time all she did was draw.

At recess she had no one to play with so she played with kindergarten kids. She thought it was the best time she ever had even though she was in grade six. After a full day of drawing in every class, the last bell rang and it was time to go home.

She saw a group of students walking together and she thought the school was going on a trip. So she followed them. At one point she heard all say 'bye' to each other and they separated. At first she was confused but then realized that they went home. Also she learned what bye means.

Her house was only 5 minutes away but it took her 2 hours to get home because she couldn't ask for directions.

That night Rachael had a lot of homework to do but she just slept because she didn't even know that she had homework.

The next day she lied to her mother that she had a stomach ache and she stayed at home. She felt so bored that the next day she went to school and tried really hard to learn English. For the whole year Rachael studied really hard and took extra English classes. Before she started grade 7 her family moved to Toronto. She had to start her new school again but this time she knew more than just 'hi.' Now Rachael can speak English and understand what people are saying to her. Sometimes she felt like going back to Korea because she thought it was really hard to learn English. But she pushed herself to the limit and things became easier for her.

Rachael
South Korea

I began to go to school on March 29, after the March Break. I was in the grade 2 in Canada. I brought a small notebook which my mother had given me. The notebook says in English, "Please, take me to the washroom, I can't speak English, I feel sick, and etc." Many classmates talked to me during the first recess. I little understood, but I was glad. Sometimes I was sad, but my teacher, Ms T., was always tender.

During lunch time, I returned home. I liked this time, because I spoke Japanese. It was very difficult to remember the names of the classmates. For example, I remembered "Moriyuki." but it was "Malik." But it seemed to be very easy for my classmates to remember my name "Ai." So, I repeatedly introduced myself in English, "My name is Ai."

I did not understand why my classmates know each other well. My elder sister told me that since they were already in the grade 2 from September last year, they know each other well. I was thinking that they were in the grade 2 with me at the same time on March 29. (Since the school year in Japan begins at April and ends at March, new class is organized in April.)

In class, I did not understand what my teacher Ms T. talked at all. I did not understand which subject I had, either. But, I thought I had to do something. I tried to copy the notebook of Lilian who was sitting next to me. Whenever I copied about 2 to 3 lines, Lilian moved to the next page.

In a math class, I could understand a little. I put up my hand, but Mrs. T. did not call on me. In a music class, I could also understand a little. I put up my hand again. Another teacher called on me. But I seemed to reply a wrong answer. One of classmates cheered me up, "You are new." "I have many things I can do," I thought.

I had many good friends. Some friends played with me without conversation, and some friends taught me English. Among them, two of my best friends always took care of me for everything. One day, they quarrelled about which took care of me. "Both of them are the best friends for me," I thought. And, I thought that I had to say something to stop them quarrelling. I said in English, "I like Maggie and Nina." They stopped quarrelling and smiled.

I like Canada, and I like Toronto. There are many peoples in Toronto, and I have many friends from many countries.

Ai

Japan

Mary was my school buddy and the only Korean student who was able to speak the language in my class. I was surprised I was in grade three because normally if I was in Korea I would be finishing the second semester of grade two. Stories my friend in Kindergarten told me about "life in Canada" were all false. Well, not necessarily all. It was true that people did not like you if you did not speak English. In that class no one was ESL and there were barely any ESL students in other grades as well. Everyone looked at me like some kind of alien, because when I spoke English, the pronunciations would be humourous. Also I was taken special care by our homeroom teacher which made other students jealous. I still think it was right for the teacher to give me that special care because I couldn't speak one word of English. I was sent to ESL classes and I learned a great deal of the language such as the format, grammar, spelling, etc.

Sara
South Korea

The first day of school had arrived and I knew no English! My mother made me go to school that day even though I was killing myself. So as I went everyone would look, point and stare. That day as I went to my first period class which was math I didn't understand anything. When she asked me if I understood anything I lied and said, "Yes." At recess no one came over to play with me. Everyone that walked by stared until finally two girls named Tajala and Somra walked over to me.

Neda
Iran

I went to school and on the first day diagnostic to check our math levels and I was the best because Iran's math is very hard but I failed the test because I didn't understand a word. A few days later I found a few Iranian friends which really helped me and I will never forget them. But lots of other people acted very brusque with me but soon I learned more and more and found more and more friends. Soon school became fun and I did learn alot of English and other stuff that year! At the end of the year we had a graduation and guess what? I won an award for the most improved student.

Arash
Iran

I lived in Albania up until I was in grade two. I left Albania and moved to Canada with my family. I came to Canada on June 3 2001. Since I came in the summer time or close to summer I didn't go to school. I met new people from Albania and the next year I went to school. My friend that I met through the summer was in my class so she helped me with my homework and explained to me what my teacher was saying to me. I didn't really understand most of the subjects. The only subject I understood was math. Math for me was easy and in my class we had a math competition on multiplication. You have to go throughout the class and answer the questions. I won the competition. I was really happy. I have changed schools for at least more than 3 times. I have got to meet alot of new people. Sometimes it was hard because I have to make new friends every time but hopefully now I won't have to if I won't move.

Ina
Albania

When I first came to Canada I thought I was going to hate it. I thought I was going to die when I got there. I didn't like it before I got there. I was crying so much and I cried when someone mentionned Mexico, my friends and my family.

On the plane my parents told me a thousand times it was going to be alright but I didn't believe them. I cried even more when I looked out the window when I was leaving my home, Mexico.

I always wanted to move to another part of Mexico City. I told my parents that I wanted to move but they didn't understand me. They always told me we would move but they never told me where.

We were on the plane for a long time but when we landed and got out of the plane I didn't feel different. I understood people because I knew a bit of English but not that much. It looked a lot like home and I couldn't really tell the difference

Once we got to the hotel I was feeling worse than before. I never knew moving could be so hard. When I looked out the window I saw people walking. I imagined my friends and walking and playing outside.

I was getting used to living in Toronto until we found another place to live. I was in the other part of the city and that's when things got crazy! I didn't get it. I thought I was moving to another city was enough. For my parents it wasn't enough. We moved from one part of the city to another until we found a building to live in.

Martha
Mexico

When I arrived at Canada I thought that I won't make any new friends or I am also worried that I would be laugh at when I say I don't know how to speak English. I was scared that my new cousins won't like me. I was also happy to meet new friends and family members. I was also scared that I won't get used to the climate. When I arrived at Canada I felt scared but after a few months I felt better.

After awhile I felt better about Canada. After a few months it started to snow so my mom thought it was some kind of bug. I also liked my new cousins and new family relatives. I also made new friends who are kind, cool and caring. I also got used to the climate and I started to play in the snow and I got a cold.

After a few years I made new friends and met new teachers. I also miss my old country and I miss my dad so much. I think that I will make more friends.

Abiram
Sri Lanka

I was in the grade 6, and I was surprised that there are many different points between the Canadian and Japanese schools.

    1. My teacher gives me notebooks, pencils and sharpeners. So, all my classmates use the same pencils. And those are all Canada-made products. In Japan, we must get our own stationeries by ourselves. And most of them are not Japan-made.

    2. Every morning, I sing Oh Canada. We have seldom sung the national anthem in Japan. So, now I can sing Oh Canada completely, whereas I can't sing our national anthem. (In Japan, the national anthem has a complicated problem, because it was used as a symbol of war before World War II. Recently, the Japanese government forced all schools to sing the national anthem, but many Japanese refuse it.)

3. Teacher drinks coffee and plays a background music during a class. Those are not possible in Japan.

4. Pupils bring snacks and cakes. And they eat them in a school. In addition, I can get ice cream in a school. To bring snacks and cakes, of course ice cream in a school is completely prohibited in Japan. So, I think Canadians get fat when they are grown up.

5. Pupils always must be drawn up in order when they enter the room and go out the room. In Japan I can come and go to the room at anytime during school days.

6. Whenever I go anywhere in school, I must go with someone (even if I go to washroom).

7. The school building is completely auto-locked.

8. There are various pupils from various countries, such as Korean, China, Russia, Mexico and Italy. But, all of them can speak English. In Japan, most of pupils are from Japan.

I did not receive any timetable and event schedule in a school. So, I do not know what I have everyday. Though my teacher might have explained tomorrow's schedule, I did not understand it. My friends kindly explained what they will have and what they had, but I barely understood them. Sometimes they explained again and again. At that time I always thought, "Please understand what I cannot understand what you say." So, I always had to watch carefully what my classmates try to do next. And when I understood it, I followed what they did.

I could understand math a little. I was very glad about it. However, since I was in the grade 5 in Japan, math in the Canadian school was advanced. I brought the math textbook to home everyday, and I prepared for the next day's lesson with my mother using English dictionary. Since I wanted to boast to my friends in Japan, I sent a copy of my math textbook which I had filled out.

When I received my report card, I was very glad to know that I got "Excellent" for math. I wore a new dress and attended the graduation ceremony. I sang Oh Canada loudly. On the last day of the school, I counted down to the completion chime with my classmates. When the school clock chimed, all my classmates cried. And, I cried too.

Yuki
Japan

Rachael
South Korea

Hinako
Japan

PROBLEMS

Not everyone made newcomers feel welcome. Some people were thoughtless and mean to them because they dressed and spoke differently. Children tell you about some of the unpleasant people they had to deal with and how they learned to stand up to bullying and racism.

Muna Shire
Stephanie Squires   **Newfoundland**
Byreona Newton
Matthew
Andrew Chung   **South Korea**
Kasim Mohamed
Michael Okran
Jaden Ai
Lester Malihan   **Philippines**

Proshat Marivani

Bullying and Racism in My Life

If it was bullying or racism it would have to be bullying. The time I got bullied was in grade four. It was a normal day at recess when I was walking around the playscape. When it was afternoon recess, this boy from nowhere was calling me fat, I did not recognize who it was so I said who is fat. He responded that I was fat. He was always at afternoon recess calling me names. Then I got so mad I chased all around school property and could not catch up. He annoyed me so much that the 2 words he said would make me snap. I had enough of him annoying me so I cried. I gave up because I had it. My classmates saw me crying and they asked, "What's the matter Muna?" I said that this kid was bothering me for a few days. I thought that I was a snitch but I felt better after. Also thought that these girls they talked to me behind my back. It was at the library. These girls maybe mentioned me by saying that,"She's not fat, she like fat." The third time that I got bullied when I was also at school. I picked out this book that was about dragons. This girl said, "Muna, I think that this book is at a advanced level. Maybe you should read a book your level." I felt that I was the worst human being of mankind. I'm sort person that when I get mentally bullied I feel like that I'm a sore loser. I have dreams that I have great friends, good grades and a good future. But in the outside it might never happen. When it might never happen, I feel like my life is gone over and there is no more in my life.

Muna

Newfie Jokes

I am here to talk to you about comedians making very hurtful Newfie jokes! My whole family was born in Newfoundland including myself, so when we hear these jokes that comedians are saying about people from Newfoundland. Examples are: "they are drunks, they are all stupid, etc..." We know the difference, but it hurts us when we see everyone laughing at the jokes. Everyone on this world has different intelligence levels, like to have fun in different ways, etc... If that is how comedians make people laugh, then I would never want that job. My family and I know what it is like to be made fun of and so do many other people! I hope one day I can stand up for not only Newfie people but for others who are getting discriminated against! Thank-you for reading my entry about discrimination in my life!

Stephanie
Newfoundland

Basket-Ball

My sister Brittany is in high school, grade 10. She is a sports fanatic and she has been since she was able to walk! She tried out for most of the teams at The Elms as well! Well anyways, my sister was having a first round tournament and my mom and I went to watch her play and cheer for her. I noticed that the population of the school was mostly African American. I was sitting on the bleachers cheering for my sister when I overheard a conversation between two boys who supposedly went to the school. There was a white teenager and a black teenager. The white one was gazing down at the court full of girls and said, "I might join the basketball team so that I can be as good as the girls." The black guy turned to him and said, "Yo, basketball is a black sport! You should try baseball!" The white guy just got up and left as some people snickered and glared at him. My mom didn't realize what had happened but I seen the whole thing. I don't think that you should have to be a certain colour to play a certain sport! It should be about your skill in the game!

Stephanie

One day I was at a program called "Gems." The program is really fun. We learn about Jesus and we do arts and crafts. One day we were doing devotions then the councillor told this girl named "Amy" to sit beside me. She gave me a dirty look and said, "I don't sit with black people or people who have black in them." The joke thing is that she never even got in trouble. I was so mad at her She never even talked to me again. I don't blame her because when she said that I pushed her. I got in trouble. That was my story on how I was in a racist situation. I hope you got a shock on how people can act about different races.

Byreona

Bullying story

The time I saw bullying was outside for recess. At recess there was a boy that was not very popular at school and because of that he got bullied a lot. That boy was I, Matthew. The things that I got bullied for were things like not being popular, being a good person and also by reporting a bad problem. An example for this is when I reported a fight that was going on at recess on school property. It involved two students throwing fists at each other. When the teachers found out what was happening they were happy that I stopped the problem. But the two students were very mad at me for reporting the problem. They called this snitching. Which was a term from the gang community I think. The students were going to beat me up. This then was the conclusion that happened to me. I'm talking about physically getting beat up by the two students. After this situation, of course they got suspended for doing this. Now I was happy that they got suspended. I say this because just for reporting something they beat me up. Which was a very bad thing. So that problem was resolved and from that day on I just walked away from those two students because I didn't want to get into a dilemma with those guys again.

Matthew

Racist Story

My racist story is about my best friend who gets bullied by a white kid because he is an Asian. So my story begins on frosty winter day when I was supposed to go to my friend's house to play. When I was outside I couldn't see him. Then I heard punches near the field and swearing from the white kid so I went over and saw my friend on the floor. He was getting bullied because he was Asian.

And he had a lot of good stuff. He told me in class they stuck dirty finger signs at him, threw notes saying threatening things to him like that if he told the teacher he was going to get killed. It had a picture of him hanged. So he was always too afraid to tell a teacher.

So that day they stole his Timberland boots, his Mp3, also his playing cards that he brought to play with. So while walking to his house the bully threw a snowball at his face and he was crying to his house. So I followed him and told his mom what happened when she asked me, "What's wrong with him?" So I told her a white boy was picking on him because he was an Asian and how he got all his stuff stolen from the kid. So his mom and me went to the principal of the school, told her everything we knew and the principal called the parents of the boy and then he was expelled from the school for lots of stuff that he did. He gave all the stuff back that he stole from my friend and then he had to apologize in front of the whole school and especially my friend. Then he learned his lesson because he had a sad face on and he held a folder, which said, "JUVENILE SCHOOL FOR KIDS AT LEAST AGE 12!"

Then he was happy for at least the rest of the day when he came to me after school.

He showed me a note that was left from the boy. The said, "Dear _____ , I am not sorry you got your butt kicked by me. I'm still going to hunt you down and kill you. I'm going to get my gang and get them to shoot you! I hate you! You little @#$%^&*!" So I kept thinking in my head, why would he say the nasty stuff about us? Just because we were grade 1's and he was a grade 6 doesn't mean he have to say those things to us. He made us real mad. So we showed the note and the teacher said that not to worry he wasn't going to do that stuff to us. Who would be mean enough to be bad to us? What would we do if the boy really did come after us? Well until then I am happy.

Andrew
South Korea

I'm going to talk about a time that I was judged badly because I'm black.

All my life I lived in Toronto until two years ago. Toronto is a multicultural place that's why I hardly see racism. Two years ago my family and me moved to Edmonton, Alberta with my cousins. The first of day I went to my new classroom. When I looked at everyone in my classroom I realized that I was the only one in my class that is black. When it was recess time everyone was looking at me and then whispering to their friends. Later on that year I was at a store near my school when I wanted to buy some candy. There were two people in the store, one was at the cashier place and the other guy was following me. I asked the guy why he was following me. Then he just looks away. When he left he was spying on me from in between the shelves. I got mad at him and I just left the store. The next day at school I was walking. Then I accidentally bumped into a boy. He started swearing at me so I just got in a fight with him. I got suspended for a week. When I returned to school he next day the same boy wanted start a problem with me. I decided that I'd do the right thing and just walk away. When it was the summer break I moved back to Toronto because I got into too much fights. When I moved to Toronto everything was back to normal.

Kasim

BULLYING RAP

This word bullying must become history,
So when people think of it will be a mystery

Bullying really must come to a stop,
Because if you don't you know you'll get dropped

Bullies think their gangsters all big and bad,
But really inside they're very sad

Bullies never get any were in life,
So when they get older they won't think rite.

Bullies always pick on the little guy's,
But when they're being bullied they'll cry.

Bullies really need to think straight,
Because if they don't they'll never appreciate

What will bullies do when they get older,
For there jobs they'll be tissue holders

Bullies think there hard with there guns,
But you know what I say that's no fun

Bullies will never go to university or college,
Because there to dumb and have no knowledge

Bullies should change while there still young,
Because if they don't they might get gunned

What will bullies do when there kicked out of there house,
 They'll Live outside in the cold like a poor lonely mouse

Bullies are always getting into stupid fights,
That's why every time there always uptight.

Now that my bullying rap has come to a stop,
All the hatred and bullying must drop.

Kasim

Dr. Martin Luther King Jr.

I think it was hard to live for black people back then because there were stores they couldn't go into, clubs they couldn't join, and sports they couldn't play. It was all because they were black. It was hard for kids to have fun because the white children were not allowed to play with black children. If I was living back then, I would try to change some people from being racist. I know I can't change everyone's thoughts about black people but I could change some. If I was living at the time of Dr. Martin Luther King Jr. I would ignore everything that people said about black people. I would treat people the way I wanted to be treated. Today I am happy that I live in a multicultural city like Toronto. There are a lot of people here from different cultures and no one treats you bad just because of your skin colour.

Michael

I have a dream!

Martin Luther King was a man who fought for his rights and didn't stop until he achieved his goal. He fought for an America where black people were allowed to do the same things as white people. In the end, the rules for black people changed and they were given equal rights. If I lived back then I would try to fix things and do something to create support like Martin did. We can create peace by standing up for people, even when they are picked on. Racism is never good so I would never allow a person to be picked on because of their skin colour. I hope for peace everyday for the rest of my life. Racism is never good.

Jaden

I have a dream

I felt sad that everyone back then was racist and bad for the innocent people who got injured or killed. If I was there I would say 'stop the violence and start the peace', 'hands are not for violence, use the kindness inside of you.' Sometimes people have a habit of saying bad words. To keep spreading peace, I would explain to people why they should be nice and kind. When I have a family, I would tell my sons/daughters to be kind and nice. Spread the peace and remove the violence.

Lester
Philippines

Proshat

FeeLINGS

The more children became used to what was happening around them, the more they came to like their new home. They tell you what it has meant for them to grow up in a strange country that finally became familiar. Now they are the ones who try to help newcomers feel at home.

Eva Bitri	**Albania**
Ziyi Cheng	**China**
Michelle Li	**China**
Brian Wu	**China**
Akshay Galia	**India**
Sara Jang	**South Korea**
Fahma	**Somalia/Italy**
Padina Abmadieh-Bondar	**Iran**
Miraj Patel	**India**
Sunghoon Hong	**South Korea**
Qasim Barlas	**United States**
Edward Chow	**Vietnam**
Zainab Pathan	**India**
Celine Ooi	**Malaysia**
Prajesh Pandya	
Amal Ahmed	**Egypt**
Nazia Zaman	**Bangladesh**
Sidra Amjed	**Pakistan**
Sara Jang	**South Korea**
Wenbin Jiang	**China**

My Family

My family and I came to Canada from Albania in 1999. Here is my story:

When my parents came to Canada, they had many struggles. One of them was that the language was totally different. They had to start a new life and they had to leave their mom, dad, brothers and sisters behind. They had to get new jobs. They also had to go to college or university if they wanted good career. My parents came here because they wanted me to grow up in a better environment. Getting used to Canada was hard but as time passed my parents got more used to the country.

Now that many years has passed my parents learned the language, finished college and university and got good jobs. I really believe in the saying, "Anything can happen if you believe. That's my story about my parents coming to Canada, I hope you enjoyed it. And remember no goal is impossible. Thank you and Good bye!

Eva
Albania

I enjoy to play computer because I found out that is really fun. My mom and dad have warned me so much times that I shouldn't go online too much, and I promised too, but still, I couldn't help myself! Other times, I'm reading which is another thing of my favourite, I'm always there to read a book and read my favourite book over and over again and I didn't see anything wrong with that. Last and the best of my favourite is school! I think going to school is so fun! I get to play with all my friends and learn new and very interesting stuff that I never know. The thing that I MOST and ONLY dislike to do was going to the mall or shopping. I always have to do something that I like to do, for example if I'm reading the greatest book in the world and suddenly my mom asks me to go to shopping, I would say a certainly NO. I know that's kind of rude but one is I'm enjoying something great and suddenly I need to do something that I really dislike I would really be really... no the other reason is I'm lazy, I don't even want to move. So that is all about me and I am the only Ziyi in the whole world, different than everyone.

Ziyi
China

I have good news. I have learned swimming, skating, making stuff and many other things in Canada and I'm in figure skating this July. My mom is right. I sure do have a better life in Canada better than China and if I never went to Canada I would never never never had the good things that happened in Canada after all, I guess.

Michelle
China

We have been in Canada for a half year now. We bought our own house. I learned a lot of English but not good enough. I spent my first Halloween and Christmas here in my first half year in Canada. It was just great. We had to wear Halloween costumes in order to get candies from each house. And we also got a lot of gifts during Christmas time. I feel very happy.

Brian
China

One of the things that I really miss about India is going all over Gujarat with my Dad because he was a Civil Engineer, and I miss looking at the things he built. They always called me Little Boss and my dream was to continue my Dad's job because he was the manager of the company.

Another thing I will never forget is that my Mom's brother was in politics and I would visit him everyday, and at night he would always take me out somewhere. However, here in Canada my parents are always tired from their jobs.

Now I have lived here for about three years and I am fully settled, and in fact I just went to India a couple of months ago to visit my Grandfather, Grandmother and the rest of my relatives. When I went back it was like going back home. I felt really happy, but I could not have imagined how much India had changed in the last few years. However, when it was time to leave again it was not that hard because this time I knew where I was going to stay, but it was still hard.

I hope you learned something about my experiences of leaving India, and here now I have such a great teacher, Mr. Whillans, and lots of friends. I feel like this is my home.

Akshay
India

I think I am completely over the stupid loser Sara because now I am able to write in full paragraphs, speak to people and I have many friends. I think the most significant proof which shows that I am adapted to Canada is that I was elected as a Student Council Executive Member, President of Doncrest Public School. Working in this spot made me remember back to the first days of school here in Canada now that I became such a strong student compared to how I was back then. Also I feel gratified now to think my goal for learning English is successfully achieved and that my parents aren't anxious about going back to Korea anymore.

Sara
South Korea

In my spare time I like to read and write. I especially I love to sing. That is of one of my special talents. My family were immigrants from Somalia. They came to Canada together in 1990. But before they came to Canada they went to Italy and spent four years there. One year later they had a miracle... ME!! I am Somalian. My religion is Muslim. We have a special month. In the month of Ramadan we fast for 30 days. After fasting for 30 days we have Eid, a time with happiness that you spend with our family and friends to laugh and smile. So there you have it my life story.

Fahma
Somalia/Italy

I never really understood why we moved here in the first place but now that I am old enough to understand social issues, I am very glad to be here. Canada is a free country with a lot of advantages and good things. The best part of it is being free to make your own choices and live life the way you want to. I like everything about Canada put aside the weather which is like a rollercoaster with a lot of twists and turns.

Padina
Iran

When I Came to Canada

It was one of the most wonderful moments in my life when I came to Canada from my home country, India. On one side I was feeling sad leaving my home, my school, my friends and on the other side I was excited of entering a new country and the new world. Everything seemed to be exciting and different to me. Starting from the airport and travelling to my house in Canada all looked like a dream to me. The roads, the cars, the high buildings, the weather, the people, the language, almost everything except my father who was as loving as ever when I saw him at the airport after 2 months. I found everything in Canada really interesting.

The first thing that thrilled me was the weather of Canada. Although I landed in the summer time, I did not feel hot. My home country, India, is considered to be one of the hottest countries in the world. The temperature over there goes as high as 52 degrees Celsius in the summer whereas Canada is totally reverse of that. Here the weather is chillier. In fact I love chillier climate than hot.

I was having difficulty in speaking English during my starting days but the teachers and friends helped me in improving my language. Now I am proud to speak as well as the people here in Canada.

I have made alot of friends after coming to Canada. All my friends belong to a different community and came from a different part of the world. It is good to learn the culture of different communities. This is the only country, I believe, where we can get this opportunity.

The only thing I probably miss is my favourite sport cricket. Although there are a couple of friends with whom I play this sport but I feel nervous to know that there are very few people here who like to play this sport in this country. But I still enjoy playing some Canadian sports like hockey.

Miraj
India

When I first came two things very surprised me. First time and weather. When I arrived it was summer and it was 9.23 p.m. However when I look out the window it was so bright it felt like 7.30 p.m. I have never seen the snow like this before. I loved snow but not any more. I hate shovelling the snow out of my driveway. And it is so cold my body keeps on freezing. In Korea I didn't have these many cold days. So it took a while to get used to this weather.

Now I am happy that my family made this choice. I have many wonderful friends and I think I could use proper English. I like this school so much and I like the teachers too. I am living very wonderful life now.

Sunghoon
South Korea

Hi my name is Qasim and I came from America when I was 6. It was year 2000 when I arrived. I felt kind of nervous because I didn't know anyone. The difference is because in America I did not feel so safe because there was a lot of violence there. There is many robbery and shooting there. I feel more safe here.

Qasim
United States

Coming To Canada

When I was in Vietnam I like Canada because my mom said Canada has snow. When I was in Vietnam I was thinking, "Is Canada cold?" because we don't have winter in Vietnam. So I think is Canada cold or not?

"Ha, did you say we need to go to Canada?"

"Yes," said my sister.

I was sad and I couldn't sleep. I was thinking is my mom and dad sad? My friends too? I was sad too. I felt sad because I have a mom, dad, dog and friends in Vietnam. If I could go back to Vietnam for one day and come back one day later I would.

This is about me and my two sisters coming to Canada so this is a sad story not a happy one. It's too bad that my dog, my friends and my parents couldn't come.

Edward
Vietnam

I came from India about two years ago. When I was in India I thought in Canada there was lots and lots of snow. There would be no summer. My friends were sad because I was going away. When I was in the airplane I felt excited and sad. I felt sad because I have my grandparents in India and I felt excited because I was coming to Canada. I would be able to meet my cousins and I would have new friends.

When I arrived here I felt like I never wanted to go to India again. I miss my grandparents but they have come to Canada to visit and sometimes my dad goes to India to visit too.

I feel very happy because I have a family, my teacher and my friends here in Canada.

Zainab
India

How I Felt Two Years Later in Canada

After two years in Canada I felt great! Canada is a wonderful country. I like Canada more than Malaysia because I don't have to worry about robbers and scary things. But I still like Malaysia because it's my home country. I am learning lots of new things in Canada. It's great to be in a new country and learn new things.

Celine
Malaysia

Today I am happy by living in Canada because it is the perfect country with a large community of my people. It is also a quiet country because it has no nuisance like the rest of the countries and no porosity. So I like Canada because it is a perfect country to live in.

Prajesh

I would like to return to my home country because all my relatives are there, and I was never away from them. So it was kind of difficult. But I still go and visit them in summer. I wouldn't really like to live in Egypt because of school. We get a lot of homework in Egypt.

But now my family and I got our Canadian citizenship. So now I am half Canadian and half Egyptian. I feel like Canada is my country. I really like it here...snow, school, my friends and everything.

Amal
Egypt

I came to Canada almost two years ago from Bangladesh so I remember every little detail clearly. It was an experience filled with mixed emotions with some feelings that cannot be written down.

At the Dhaka International Airport my grandparents and my aunt were the only ones there because everyone else had to be at work for which I was sad but I was glad too because it would've been harder for me to leave, having to say goodbye to so many family members. When I said goodbye for the last time and got on the plane, I felt a sudden emptiness inside, which was soon filled with the excitement of going to another country, starting a new life. My mom said it would be hard for us to start all over but she told us to stay strong and we did.

Life in Canada was weird at first being all alone with my older brother while our parents worked but that's what got us closer together. Now we tell each other things that we don't even tell our Mom or Dad.

Canada is a very good country to live in and it is very peaceful. My first snow day with my friends at school was an unforgettable moment. School in Canada is a lot better than school in Bangladesh because the teachers there are much

121

harsher. The first month of school was very quiet but I made friends the second month. Everyone accepted me the way I was and I didn't have to change. These are just a few things I could tell you about living in Canada.

I have met new people and now they are my best friends. Canada is very different from Bangladesh which is good in some matters. But I still miss my old country because of my friends and relatives. Canada will never be like Bangladesh for me. It will always be a foreign country for me because it doesn't have my family, doesn't have that feeling of being at home. It will always have the feeling of being away from home and my loved ones.

I hope you can understand what I feel about coming to Canada and leaving Bangladesh.

Nazia
Bangladesh

I learned how to speak English very fast. When I finally did find some friends I knew how to speak English. After a little while I learned how to make new friends. So now I could make lots of friends. Now that I know how to speak English, I can stand up for myself. So if some one does call me names or makes fun of me, I can say, "Hey, so what if I come from Pakistan! Do you have a problem with it?" I also spoke English with my brothers. So I get practice at home as well as at school. Since I can speak English and stand up for myself, nobody makes fun of me anymore.

Now I really like Canada. I have more friends here than in Pakistan. I learned lots of new things, like a new language, tried lots of new food and lots of other things. My family likes to live in Canada just like me. We also call our family back in Pakistan, like uncles, aunts and other relatives. Then we share what we have to say. Canada is a great place to stay.

Sidra
Pakistan

Sara
South Korea

Wenbin
China

afterword

Because Canada is a country where freedom is cherished, it is no wonder that the families of the children whose letters you have read have come here. The children have written about why they came and what they had to leave behind. Through their own words and artwork you have learned a little of the pain they felt leaving dear people and familiar places and the challenges they faced while trying to fit into the foreign conditions of a new home and a new life. Going to school eventually brought friends and a new language that set them on their way to becoming educated members of the Canadian society. This book could not have happened without their dedicated teachers who connected us to them.

As an author, Emily Hearn has been mentoring the creative writing skills of such students in the public school system; as a teacher, Marywinn Milne has worked with ESL/ESD (English as a Second Language/Dialect) students for more than thirty years. This is where we heard these voices.

One of the students in Marywinn's first Grade 2 class was a young boy from Vietnam who had escaped by boat and had found refuge with his family in Canada. When he acquired enough English to finally be able to tell his story, she was amazed at his journey and knew then that she wanted to become an ESL teacher to help students adjust to life in Canada. She found that as soon as students had enough English to carry on a limited conversation they were eager to talk about their country, family, customs, and what they like or disliked about their new home. In her early years, there were not many materials to work with, but a book called *Come With Us* (Women's Press) was very helpful. In the thirty years since then, children have arrived from many more countries and have shown the same eagerness to share all that has happened to them.

Canada was founded by immigrants. Emily Hearn's own father came to Canada as a little boy, sent with his brother from England by Barnardo Homes at the beginning of the 20th century. Her mother's grandmother came from England in 1830 at the same time as her grandfather's people moved north from Lancaster, Pennsylvania and founded what became Kitchener, Ontario. Emily's husband's family came much earlier, in the late 1600s as Huguenots escaping religious constrictions in France. His mother's relatives were from Ireland and Scotland. Our population has always been a grand mix and as you see, it continues to be.

We hope that it has been instructive for you to hear their own voices as today's immigrant children describe the momentous changes in their young lives. And perhaps with this book, their words and images have opened the doors to a new understanding of the courage, spirit, and perseverance it has taken for them to adjust to their new home.

Emily Hearn
Marywinn Milne

acKNOWLeDGMeNTS

The editors would like to thank the teachers and students of the
following schools who have so enthusiastically contributed to
this project:

Albion Heights JMS; Calico PS; Coppard Glen PS; C.R. Marchant
MS; Daystrom PS; Dixon Grove JMS; Doncrest PS; Finch PS;
George Anderson PS; North Kipling JMS; Palmerston PS; Queen
Victoria PS; Sheppard PS; Smithfield MS; Stilecroft PS; The Elms
JMS; Topcliff PS; Willowdale MS; Woburn PS.